THE
LYNTON &
BARNSTAPLE
RAILWAY
REMEMBERED

J. D. C. A. Prideaux

DAVID & CHARLES
NEWTON ABBOT LONDON NORTH POMFRET (VT)

British Library Cataloguing in Publication Data

Prideaux, J.D.C.A.
The Lynton & Barnstaple Railway remembered.
— 2nd ed.
1. Lynton & Barnstaple Railway — Pictorial
works
I. Title   II. Lynton & Barnstaple Railway
album
385′.52′0942352   HE3821.L9

ISBN   0–7153–8958–0

First published as *Lynton & Barnstaple Railway Album*,
1974; this edition published 1989

Photoset and Printed in Great Britain by
Redwood Burn Limited, Trowbridge, Wiltshire
for David & Charles Publishers plc
Brunel House Newton Abbot Devon

Published in the United States of America
by David & Charles Inc
North Pomfret Vermont 05053 USA

Contents

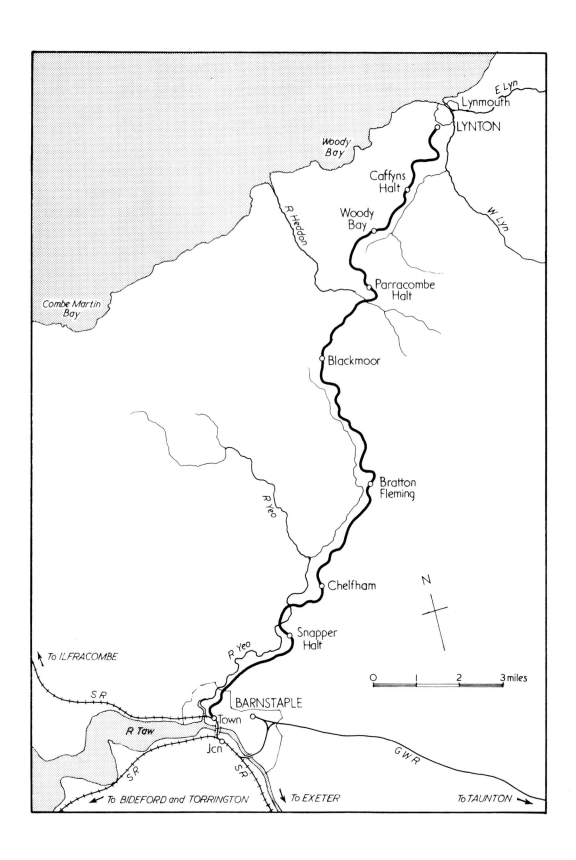

Introduction

The Lynton and Barnstaple Railway ran from Barnstaple across the foothills of Exmoor to terminate at the top of a cliff above Lynton. The narrow gauge of 1ft 11½in was chosen following its successful use on the Festiniog Railway, as a means of building a line which could economically carry the limited amount of traffic available in this deeply rural area. Not that the narrow gauge was used as an excuse for light construction or low standards. Track, structures and rolling stock were all excellent without being elaborate.

Perhaps it was the combination of a first class railway and a glorious setting that gave the line its appeal and which still attracts interest all these years later. It was the familiar branch line on a small scale – and for much of its life it was independent. All very English. Where else did you find a company in serious financial straights whose directors would instruct their engineer to build culverts to allow deer a chance of escape when hunted? Or for that matter, a railway where a first-class passenger scattered flower seeds from the window to make the route more beautiful?

After a series of abortive schemes the Lynton & Barnstaple Railway Act received the Royal Assent on 27 June 1895. All the directors were local figures, and it was the chairman's wife, Lady Newnes, who cut the first sod at the site of Lynton station in September of that year. Construction took a year longer than expected and the disputes which arose with the contractor caused financial problems which the company never really shook off. The railway eventually opened on 11 May 1898.

There were few major changes until the Southern Railway bought the line in 1923. The big company decided on a programme of major improvements. Much work was done on the track. A new locomotive, cranes, and wagons were bought and put into service between 1925 and 1927. Commendable

though this effort was it did not take much account of the railway's potential traffic needs. Lower investment directed towards reducing operating costs would have had a better chance of avoiding, or at least postponing, closure, which came on 29 September 1935. The last train was a special excursion attended by all the carnival scenes which have more recently become associated with such occasions.

Unlike many other narrow gauge railways the L&B was not dominated by any one particular traffic. In better years, when independent, it carried roughly 100,000 passengers and 8,000 tons of freight a year. The heaviest single traffic was coal, which in early days arrived by coaster at the railway's own wharf. The variety of freight moved by train in those days was very considerable – as can be seen in the photographs. Two coaches generally sufficed for passengers – except on Barnstaple market days and during the peak summer tourist season.

In independent days, the line had a basic winter service of three trains daily. The first train down, around 6.20am, carried overnight mail and newspapers from London. Returning from Lynton it made a connection with the main London express, the Alexandra (later known as the Atlantic Coast Express). The next down train ran on alternate days at 10.00am or 11.30am, and the third down train followed at about 4.00pm, providing a connection from London. There was always an additional train on Fridays – Barnstaple market day. During the summer the service was augmented to give five, six and sometimes seven trains each way.

The Southern altered the basic service by dividing the mail and newspaper train into two portions; in the final timetable one left Barnstaple at 5.33am and the second at 7.00am – neither of which can have been of much use to passengers. The SR also included an 'as required' freight service in one timetable. It was not repeated which is sufficient comment in itself. As with investment, the big company tried, but got little return for its effort.

This book was originally published in 1974 as *The Lynton and Barnstaple Railway Album*. This new edition has been revised, reset, and includes a number of different and extra photographs. The Album itself followed a history *The Lynton & Barnstaple Railway* (David & Charles) written jointly with Gordon Brown and Harry Radcliffe which provides a detailed account of the railway to anyone tempted to delve further.

The L&B was particularly fortunate in its photographers. There is a magnificent album taken while the line was under construction. Later a local firm, R. L. Knight & Co attended many of the occasions. Several well known railway photographers visited the line including H. L. Hopwood, F. E. and D. H. Box, K. A. C. R. Nunn (collection now held by the Locomotive Club of Great Britain) A. B. MacLeod, H. G. W. Household, H. C. Casserley, S. W. Baker, H. F. Wheeller and J. G. Dewing. I am very grateful to all the photographers whose work appears in the book. I should also like to thank J. B. Hollingsworth for putting his collection at my disposal and to the retired railwaymen and their relatives at Barnstaple who went to so much trouble to dig up photographs and information for me – in particular F. Trott, Mrs S. Liley and Gordon Walters.

Right: The Lynton & Barnstaple Railway coat of arms.

Overleaf: On 17 September 1895 Lady Newnes 'honoured the directors by cutting the first sod' at the site of Lynton Station. *(The late S. Liley)*

Below: An engraving showing *Exe* as built.
(The Engineer)

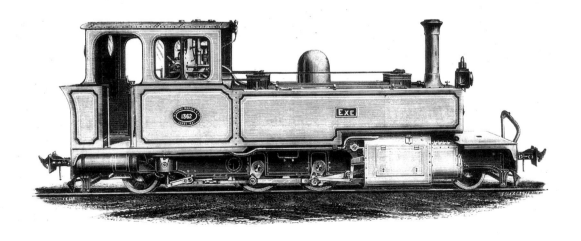

CONSTRUCTION

Above: The Lynton & Barnstaple was dogged by the initial disputes between the company and its contractor. The contractor anticipated being able to build a surface line and was horrified at the number of rock cuttings, like the one shown here in a 1927 double-headed scene. (H. G. W. Household)

Left: One of the rock cuttings which caused the contractor such trouble and expense – the railway opened a year late and the contractor was bankrupted.
(North Devon Athenaeum)

Right upper: The construction of the railway started in the spring of 1896 and took two years – twice as long as anticipated. At least three locomotives were used with unconfirmed reports of other locomotives at obscure points on the line. In this early view *Excelsior* is shown with a spoil train. (North Devon Athenaeum)

Right lower: *Excelsior* was a diminuitive wing-tank, built originally by W. G. Bagnall for the Kerry Tramway in Mid-Wales. In this view she is shown after the balloon stack originally fitted had been replaced by a straight stove pipe. (L&GRP)

Above: Horses as well as locomotives were used by the contractor. This photograph shows the early stages of the construction of the big bank at Parracombe. Like most other photographs taken before the opening of the railway it comes from a fascinating album in the North Devon Athenaeum. While the original source of these photographs is not now known, it seems likely that they were taken for Mr E. B. Jeune – a prominent local resident and a director of the company.

(North Devon Athenaeum)

Right upper: A view of the completed road bed where it crossed Mill Leat on the outskirts of Barnstaple. Unfortunately the identity of the people who pose so confidently is unknown. Note the solid construction of the permanent way, which consisted of 40lb/yd rail in 30ft lengths, spiked to wooden sleepers at 2ft 6in centres

(North Devon Athenaeum)

Right lower: Collar (or Collard) Bridge marked the point about 3½ miles from Barnstaple where the line climbed out of the Yeo Valley and started on the long ascent at 1 in 50 which lasted until Blackmoor. The name was variously applied to this bridge and to the adjacent river bridge. The line is nearly complete in this photograph. The track still needs lifting and packing and the fencing is incomplete. Enough land was bought to allow the line to be doubled – if necessary.

(North Devon Athenaeum)

The major engineering work on the line was Chelfham Viaduct, which consisted of eight arches built of Marland brick on masonry piers. The views on these pages show the various stages in the construction of the viaduct from starting the piers to testing by the contractor's locomotives *Slave* and *Kilmarnock*.

(North Devon Athenaeum)

Right upper: Two days later on Wednesday 16 March, 1898 the company entertained Press representatives who travelled to Lynton behind *Yeo*, driven by Driver Pilkington and Fireman Willis. The photograph shows the party at Lynton before their return, and, after lunch at the Manor House. *(North Devon Athenaeum)*

Below: The first train ran through to Lynton on 14 March 1898. At that stage much of the contractor's equipment remained in evidence.
(North Devon Athenaeum)

Right lower: Several other runs were made for publicity, to establish operating schedules, and for inspection. No details of the one shown here seem to have survived, but it clearly pre-dated the erection of signalling equipment at Lynton. Note the absence of signal posts and the position of the two points in the crossover. In practice most trains ran mixed, with freight and passenger vehicles, and the crossover shown in this picture was soon reversed to make operation easier.
(North Devon Athenaeum)

Above: Undoubtedly a publicity shot. The train is specially formed from the two first saloon brakes and two of the four third-class coaches with an open observation portion in the centre. The blower seems to be hard on to produce a most unrealistic amount of steam for a stationary train. The locomotive is *Yeo*, the location is the Yeo Valley and the date, early 1898.
(North Devon Athenaeum)

Right: 'Trolleying down after inspection' is the original caption for this photograph – but where, or which inspection is unknown. *(North Devon Athenaeum)*

Below: The reporters' train at Woody Bay.

BARNSTAPLE TOWN

Above: Barnstaple Town was a joint station with the London & South Western Railway and the busiest point on the line. This photograph, which again comes from the North Devon Athenaeum Album and pre-dates the opening, is taken from the River Taw and looks across the standard gauge line to the station building and the Lynton & Barnstaple platform. *(North Devon Athenaeum)*

Below: Another view of the new station taken from the narrow gauge platform. The LSWR Ilfracombe line platform is on the right, and the rail and road bridges crossing the Taw towards Barnstaple Junction Station can be seen in the background. *(North Devon Athenaeum)*

Above: The opening on 11 May 1898 was a very festive occasion with Barnstaple Corporation arriving at the Town Station in procession. Nevertheless it is not the civic dignitaries who took pride of place in this photograph. *(North Devon Athenaeum)*

Below: Staff at Barnstaple Town before the first world war. *(J.D.C.A. Prideaux collection)*

BARNSTAPLE TOWN
CHANGE HERE FOR
LYNTON & LYNMOUTH

Above: Photographs showing standard and narrow gauge trains together at the Town station are very rare. In this 1935 view by S. W. Baker the N class 2–6–0 on an Ilfracombe train completely dwarfs *Lew* and her train waiting to leave for Lynton. *(S. W. Baker)*

Below: Looking the other way, *Taw* arrives at Barnstaple on the 12.15 from Lynton on 7 September 1933. Note the platform wagon, one of two built in 1902, and the transfer siding in front of the trees in the distance. *(K. A. C. R. Nunn)*

Above: Nowadays it is difficult to visualise the great variety of traffic handled by railways over short distances 50 years or so ago. Here *Lew* and one of the other Manning Wardle 2–6–2Ts wait to leave on a train conveying coal, hay, a van load of parcels and several passenger coaches. *(H. G. W. Household)*

Below: In the later years of the line's existence, the 10.15 from Barnstaple was a popular train in the summer months for day visitors to Lynton and was often double-headed. This photograph of *Taw* and *Yeo* in 1935 was probably of this train. *(A. B. MacLeod)*

Above: A quite delightful view of *Taw* being coaled at the exchange siding at Barnstaple Town. The line visible just behind the engine is the main line curving away to Pilton Yard, and the presence of circus vans suggests that it is September and Barnstaple Fair time.

(J. G. Dewing)

Right upper: The railway approaches to towns are rarely particularly attractive, and the Lynton & Barnstaple was no exception. Here we look back towards Barnstaple Junction with the signal box just visible behind the warning notice. *(H. G. W. Household)*

Right lower: Braunton Road Crossing. The road was so much wider than the narrow track bed that the gates lapped each other when closed against the railway. One of the only two fatal accidents to occur on the line took place here in March 1910 when W. H. Hart, a platelayer, was killed opening the crossing gates. The siding to the wharf on the River Yeo, much used for coal from South Wales before World War I, branched off from the point where the photographer stood.

(H. G. W. Household)

Right upper: Lew at Pilton 17 June, 1926. *(H. C. Casserley)*

Below: Pilton Yard at Barnstaple was the operating headquarters of the railway with offices, workshops, locomotives and carriage sheds, goods sidings and a turntable. *Taw* is shunting coaches into carriage shed No 2 in this photograph, taken on 15 July 1935. The locomotive sheds with workshop behind are on the left and the freight yard to the right behind the engine.

(S. W. Baker)

Right lower: Taw and *Exe* inside Pilton shed in June 1926. *(H. C. Casserley)*

The Lynton & Barnstaple had its share of minor derailments. In these photographs taken around 1922 one of the bogies from eight-ton van No 23 has derailed near Snapper and passengers are being ferried from each side of the block by relief trains. Nobody seems to mind, however, and the hats are a historical feature in themselves! At this period, before the Southern improved the track, it was common practice for a platelayer to ride on the train in hot weather. *(R. L. Knight)*

Overleaf; pages 30/1 and 32/3: Two very fine photographs showing *Yeo* and *Lew* on trains near Snapper Halt in 1935 appear on the following pages. *(The Times)*

CHELFHAM

Above: Lew runs in across the viaduct in a wintery scene, towards the end of the railway's life. *(D. E. H. Box)*

Right upper: An earlier view, looking north, aroun 1920. *(L&GR*

Right lower: It was normal to take water at Chelfhar This unusual view shows *Lew* in 1935. *(A. B. MacLeo*

ACCIDENT

The worst accident in the company's history occurred
at Chumhill in 1913. Four men were travelling on
wagon No 10 loaded with ballast, running by gravity
from Bratton Fleming to Chelfham, the brakes failed to
hold and the wagon came off on a reverse curve killing
two of the men. The photographs show various stages
in the recovery operation.   *(R. L. Knight)*

BRATTON

Spring and autumn in the Bratton Valley. These two photographs showing trains hauled by *Taw* and *Lyn* near Bratton Fleming were published in the earlier book *The Lynton & Barnstaple Railway* but justify republishing in the larger page size of this volume. The date seems to be around 1933 as the locomotives have been fitted with steam heating and eight-ton vans still retain diagonal cross-bracing which had been replaced with angle-iron before the railway closed. It was usual to marshal wagons at the front of down trains except when steam heating was in use.   *(D. E. H. Box)*

Lynton and Barnstaple Railway.

Refer hereto in	General Manager's Office,	To	In reply to your
3/1032.	Barnstaple, A	Mr. Fursdon.	
your reply.	7th July, 1913	Lynton.	

K. D. S. Ltd.—K 4150.

NOTICE TO ALL CONCERNED.

Special Rates (Passenger Train) with
Birmingham for Rabbits, &c.

Please note & record that the rate of 4/3d per cwt. recently
advised is at Owner's Risk.

Above: The photograph was taken in 1927, but is almost indistinguishable from views taken in 1898. In 1931, however, the line nearest the camera was lifted and the yard connection put in the former up line.

(H. G. W. Household)

Below: Yeo at Bratton in 1935 on a train for Barnstaple

(A. B. MacLeod)

Right upper: A view, unusual since it does show Bratton goods yard. Four-wheeled and bogie coal wagons are in evidence, and the track bed from the siding, removed in 1931, can be seen behind the contractor's tip wagon. *(A. B. MacLeod)*

LYNTON & BARNSTAPLE RAILWAY.

Manager's Office,
July 7th.1913.

Increase of Rates by Passenger Train. LOCAL Traffic.

With the exception of the under mentioned rate the local traffic scales & rates will NOT be increased —

Rate for Rabbits (dead). — To be increased from 6d to 7d per cwt., minimum weight, 1 cwt., as at present. — *between any L+B station + Barnstaple*

Please acknowledge receipt.

C.E.Drewett.

Above: Lancey Brook viaduct was a curving structure of steel spans and masonry piers; it was a less impressive and less accessible structure than Chelfham and the author does not know of any photographs of it taken during the period when the railway was open. This rather intriguing view shows an inspection trolley on the viaduct during construction. *(North Devon Athenaeum)*

Lynton and Barnstaple Railway.   UP.

Engine Driver's Report.   24ᵗʰ day,   Aug   1901,   8·55 A.m. Train.

STATIONS.	SERVICE TIME. Arrival. H.	M.	Departure. H.	M.	ACTUAL TIME. Arrival. H.	M.	Departure. H.	M.	VEHICLES ATTACHED. Coaches.	Goods. Brake Vans.	Goods Trucks. Loaded. Goods, 8 W.	Goods, 4 w.	Empty.	VEHICLES DETACHED. Goods Trucks. 8 W.	4 W.	REMARKS.
Lynton							8	58	3		1					
Wooda Bay					9	13	9	14								
Blackmoor					.	30	.	31								
Bratton...					.	48	.	49								
Chelfham					10	1	10	3								
Barnstaple					.	21										
										TOTAL						
										Time finished duty						

H. J. Nilli   **Driver's Signature.**

Above: North of Bratton Fleming the railway ran through hillside farms. In this evening shot *Lew* on Honeycott Bank, approaches Bratton with the 6.07 pm from Lynton on 8 September 1933. *(K. A. C. R. Nunn)*

BLACKMOOR

Blackmoor was the principal intermediate station. The prospectus confidently anticipated that many excursion passengers from Ilfracombe to Lynton would change from coach to train here but the coach proprietors did not take so kindly to this idea. With remarkable enterprise Sir George Newnes started the first railway motor coach service in April 1903 from Blackmoor to Ilfracombe, but this experiment did not prosper; to quote a local newspaper; 'one of these cars was travelling at a little over 8 mph on a high road when the police interfered, a prosecution was instituted and a heavy fine inflicted. Sir George Newnes has now decided to stop running the cars over this route'. The two coaches were then sold to the Great Western Railway which used them to found its road transport department with a service running between Helston and The Lizard. Blackmoor thus reverted to being nothing but a substantial station with an adjacent livestock market, but no surrounding buildings other than scattered farms. The photograph, below, shows one of the Miles-Daimlers at Helston. *(J. D. C. A. Prideaux collection.)*

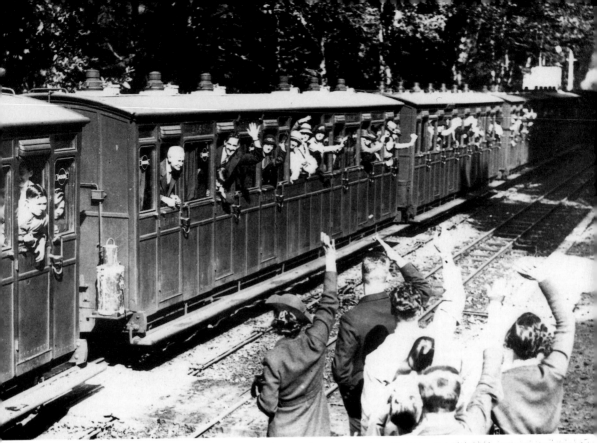

Above: The last train on its way to Lynton. At the end of the platform is the water tower; a hot air engine was housed in the stone base of this tower and used to lift water into the tank.

Right upper: A rainy day in 1927 with the down train pulling in. The track here is laid on concrete sleepers, a Southern experiment which was not repeated as they were found to be unduly noisy and lacking in resilience.
(H. G. W. Household)

Right: Leaving for Lynton – from the road bridge.
(L&GRP)

Above: An early view of Parracombe Bank. This photograph was used for a well known early postcard with one noticeable difference; on the back of the original is scrawled 'put in smoke' which, in the postcard, rather hides the view!
(*J. D. C. A. Prideaux*)

Right upper: A view of the same location just before closure. A new main road which made the railway even less competitive can be seen in the background. During the torrential rains which led to the Lynmouth flood disaster in 1952 water built up between the two embankments and the railway embankment eventually gave with results that added to the tragedy.

Right lower: The last train, headed by *Lew* and *Yeo*, swings on to Parracombe bank.
(*R. L. Knight*)

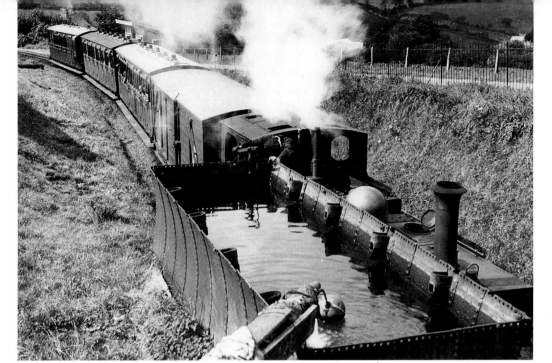

ARRACOMBE HALT

Left: Parracombe, the largest community en route, was given the least facilities. The Halt was only opened several months after the railway and initially only the Friday market trains stopped there. Tickets were issued at the local post office. This photograph of *Lyn* is taken from the bridge by St. Petrock's church. *(J. G. Hubback)*

Above: Parracombe water was particularly good for locomotive purposes. *Lew* is the engine involved on this 1935 train. *(A. B. MacLeod)*

(25)

Lynton and Barnstaple Railway.

Refer hereto in	General Manager's Office, Barnstaple,	A	To	In reply to your
3/1032.			Mr Fursdon.	
your reply.	30th July, 1913		Lynton.	

K. D. S. Ltd.—K 4150.

NOTICE TO ALL CONCERNED

Rabbit Tfc. (Dead) between L & B.Co's Stns. &
Birmingham.

The L & S.W.Co. have withdrawn their sanction & will not agree
to rabbit traffic being booked through to Birmingham, via Barnstaple
Jcn., Templecombe & Mid.Co.   Please note that the rates issued
apply only to Birmingham traffic consigned via Barnstaple & Gt.W.Co.
Traffic consigned to Birmingham, Mid. must be booked to Barnstaple
for re-entry.

Newed

Above: The church tower is partially obscured by steam from the safety valves in this photograph of *Lew* leaving Parracombe on the 3.15 pm from Barnstaple on 7 September 1933. *(K. A. C. R. Nunn)*

Below: *Lew* storms through Blackleigh cutting near Parracombe on 15 July 1935. *(S. W. Baker)*

WOODY BAY

Above: Like Blackmoor, Woody Bay (or Wooda Bay as it was originally called) was a station of expectations, in this case from an abortive scheme for a holiday resort about three miles away. A branch line was even discussed in the early days. The station was in reality situated at Martinhoe Cross and one of the few signs of potential grandeur was the station hotel.

(J. D. C. A. Prideaux collection)

Below: Yeo pauses on a down train in July 1935

(S. W. Baker)

Left upper: Exe on an up train at Woody Bay.

(Lens of Sutton)

Above: Lew arrives at Woody Bay on the 3.15 pm from Barnstaple in September 1933. The station was particularly well situated for attractive evening photographs.

(K. A. C. R. Nunn)

Left lower: One of the few photographs showing an engine shunting at an intermediate station; in this case *Exe* is running round her train at the Barnstaple end of Woody Bay Station. The signal is not original but a Southern Railway replacement. *(Lens of Sutton)*

Left upper: Just over an hour later *Taw* leaves Woody Bay on the 4.25 pm from Barnstaple. The up home signal was still the Lynton & Barnstaple installation at this stage, but had been changed to a standard Southern upper quadrant by the time the next photograph was taken. *(K. A. C. R. Nunn)*

Left lower: *Lew* on an up train enters Woody Bay Station in July 1935. *(S. W. Baker)*

Below: The summit of the line was reached just beyond Woody Bay, and engines on up trains had little to do from here to Barnstaple. This view shows *Yeo* near the summit on 15 July 1935. *(S. W. Baker)*

Above: For the last few miles into Lynton the railway followed the side of the West Lyn river valley. This early photograph near Dean Steep is unusual in that it shows a five coach train, one over the maximum for a single locomotive, except between Blackmoor and Lynton.

(J. D. C. A. Prideaux)

Right upper: Lyn drifts down towards Lynton at some unrecorded time in the middle 1920s. *(F. Box*

Right lower: The last train before closure, seen here a Dean Steep. *(R. L. Knight*

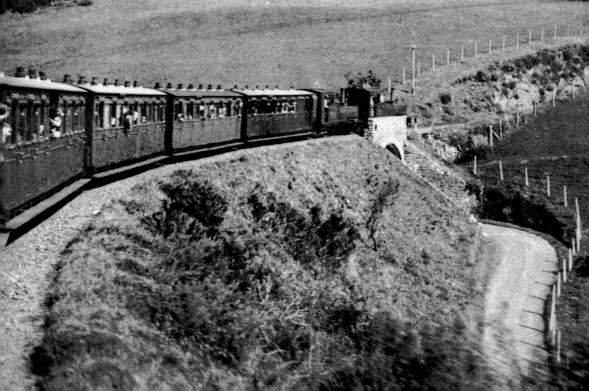

LYNTON

Left: The 1 in 50 gradient started at the platform end at Lynton, a tough climb for up trains. This early view shows a train storming through the woods at Barbrook.
(J. D. C. A. Prideaux)

Above: Taw arriving at Lynton in 1935.   *(R. L. Knight)*

Above: Lynton station was not easily accessible. The site was supposedly chosen to avoid interfering with the view of the 'twin villages'. Successful in that, it left the severe practical disadvantage of being some way from, and many many feet above, the town it should have served. No wonder the horse looks tired.

(*J. D. C. A. Prideaux*)

Overleaf: By comparison with the photograph, right, a posed photograph taken in 1935. The blower is hard on for effect – on a downgrade. The bracket signals installed by the Southern are clearly shown. *(The Times)*

Right: An early view of Lynton Station as it would have been seen by the driver of a train approaching from Barnstaple. The buildings, from right to left, are the signal box, the station building, the goods shed and office and the locomotive shed. The layout had been changed by the time this photograph was taken. Originally access to the engine shed was through a double slip where the first set of points giving access to the bay platform are shown. This double slip, a complex piece of equipment for a 1ft 11½in gauge railway can be seen dumped on the ground between the engine shed and the main line. The photograph is also interesting in showing the original home and starting signals. The home consists of two semaphore arms, one below the other although the top arm was not in the picture.

Above: A 1935 view with *Yeo* ready to leave for Barnstaple. *(A. B. Macleod)*

Right upper: Shunting in progress. *Lew* is propelling wagons through the shed while the coal road can be seen on the left. *(A. B. MacLeod)*

Previous page: The timetable occasionally required two trains to be at Lynton together. On 16 July 1935 *Lew* is about to depart, while *Taw* has arrived from Barnstaple. *(S. W. Baker)*

Right lower: The station buildings at Lynton, Wood Bay and Blackmoor were built in the so-called Swiss Chalet style. This is Lynton after the Southern had added parcels and enquiry offices. *Taw* stands at the platform. *(L & GR)*

(North Devon Athenaeum)

LOCOMOTIVES

Above: The railway started life with three locomotives. They were 2–6–2 tank engines, built by Manning Wardle & Company of Leeds in 1897 and named after local rivers, *Yeo, Exe* and *Taw. Yeo* was the first to be delivered. Presumably this was a portentous occasion, or so we would judge by the expressions on the faces of the men involved. *(North Devon Athenaeum)*

Right upper: It is difficult now to credit the standard of cleaning achieved in Edwardian days. One would imagine that the fish scale polishing shown in this picture taken on 6 July 1912 was for a special occasion were it not also found on many other photographs taken before World War I. This photograph is particularly interesting as it disproves the view previously held that cabs were altered shortly after the opening to obviate smoke collecting in the recess formed by the first side window. Later evidence suggests that this alteration took place between 1912 and 1920. *(H. L. Hopwood)*

Right lower: Exe at Lynton. The cab alteration is clearly shown.

Above: The company originally ordered three loco-motives, but realised even before the opening that this left little or no margin for emergencies, repairs or heavy traffic; accordingly it was decided to order a fourth engine in February 1898. In this case the engine was Baldwin Locomotive Works, Philadelphia USA 2–4–2T No 15965, May 1898 – or *Lyn. Lyn* arrived and was first steamed in July 1898. Here she is shown following erection at Pilton Yard. *(E. Northcombe)*

Right upper: A very early view of *Lyn* standing on th engine shed road at Lynton, when access to the she was still via the double slip. *Lyn* gave a fair amount o trouble in her early days, getting off to a bad start b melting a fusible plug on her first run. In fact, Sir Georg Newnes complained in 1903 that she had caused mo trouble and expense then the three Manning Wardle put together. At this stage a normal British smoke bo door had been fitted and the painted name covered u by a name plate. *(L&GR*

Right lower: Another photograph at Lynton during th first few years of the century. *Lyn* had been repainted standard Lynton & Barnstaple colours and had rai fitted to the coal bunker. *(L&GR*

Left upper: In 1907 *Lyn's* boiler was condemned after the inspector's hammer penetrated one of the plates, and a replacement boiler was built by Avonside. It can easily be distinguished from the original by the absence of the American ash removing equipment. Here she stands at Pilton on 6 July 1912.   *(H. L. Hopwood)*

Left lower: Another view of *Lyn* taken around the same time at Lynton.   *(J. D. C. A. Prideaux)*

Above: *Lyn* climbs past Barbrook in early SR days. During the early 1920's *Lyn's* attractive copper capped chimney was replaced by a stovepipe.   *(F. E. Box)*

Above: Lyn, final condition. With *Yeo* at Pilton.
(H. C. Casserley)

Right: Lyn, returning from overhaul, Eastleigh, January 1929.
(R. L. Knight)

Left upper: The Southern decided to order an extra locomotive, a decision difficult to understand as the L&B had always managed with four engines. *Lew* was a sister to *Yeo, Exe* and *Taw*. The major difference was the cab which avoided the smoke trap. Here she is being delivered on 30 July 1925. The scene is little different from *Yeo's* arrival 27 years earlier.

(H. C. Casserley)

Above: Lew at Pilton in 1927. Later alterations included the fitting of steam heating apparatus and extended columns to the safety valves. *(H. G. W. Household)*

Left lower: Coaling up at Pilton during the 1930s. A view showing *Yeo*, for comparison. *(J. D. C. A. Prideaux)*

COACHES

The Lynton & Barnstaple Railway Company's Directors took a personal interest in their coaching stock. Sixteen carriages were built for the opening by the Bristol Waggon & Carriage Works, and half of these, four firsts and four thirds, included open observation sections. Perhaps it was inevitable that spark guards (in practice panes of glass) would be added to the firsts after only a short time. The photographs show coach 3 (above) before the opening, and as 2473 in 1935 (below) when fitted with spark guards and converted to third. Brake composite No 2 (right) includes a dog box, this facility was not found in the third class brakes. The final photograph shows third class observation coach 2465 (formerly 7) in 1935.

(J. D. C. A. Prideaux, A. B. MacLeod, North Devon Athenaeum, A. B. MacLeod)

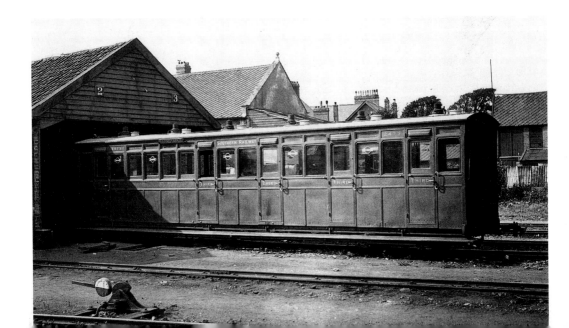

Above: The railway had two 'conventional' third brakes and four seven-compartment thirds. One of the third brakes is shown in this photograph. The non-brake vehicles were similar with the brake section replaced by a further two compartments.   *(North Devon Athenaeum)*

Right: Not a great many alterations were made to the coaches. The original oil lamps were replaced by acetylene lighting before World War I and the Southern converted Nos 3 and 4 to all third. No 15 (Southern Railway 6993) was, however, altered soon after the opening to a composite to allow it to be used in one coach trains and is shown as such in this photograph.

(H. G. W. Household)

Below: The other coaches ordered were also conventional. Composite coach No 6 seated 12 first and 32 third class passengers.   *(J. D. C. A. Prideaux)*

Above: Only one extra passenger carriage was built for the Lynton & Barnstaple, being erected at Pilton in 1903. Clearly built with a view to one coach trains it incorporated first and third, smoking and non-smoking compartments with the first smoking coupé serving as an observation compartment as well. This photograph was taken at Pilton in 1912. The amount of house building since 1898 is noteworthy. *(H. L. Hopwood)*

GOODS WAGONS

Below: The railway started with two eight-ton capaci￼ brake vans. They were clearly most useful vehicle￼ another was built by the company in 1908 at Pilton a￼ four further vans added by the Southern in 1927. Ly￼ ton & Barnstaple No 14 is shown standing at Pilt￼ before the opening of the railway. Note the provision ￼ the dog box, as in the first class brakes.

(North Devon Athenaeu￼

Above. No 23 built by the company in 1908 followed much the same pattern as the original vans. It was the only wooden framed vehicle on the line. *(L&GRP)*

Below: Four additional eight-ton vans were built by J. F. Howard of Bedford for the Southern in 1927. By that time it was clear that there was little if any call for purely freight trains and the guard's compartments were omitted. In addition to their proper use as freight and parcels vehicles, these eight-ton vans were often used for passenger luggage. *(H. G. W. Household)*

Above: The four ton, four-wheeled open goods wagons were the most numerous single type of vehicle on the line. In all eight were built for the line and No 10 poses at Pilton before the opening. *(North Devon Athenaeum)*

Right: Six four-ton goods vans were built at the same time as the open wagons and on a similar chassis. SR No 47040, shown in 1935, was originally L&BR No 15. *(A. B. MacLeod)*

Below: In the freight siding at Woody Bay stands a four-wheel open goods wagon and eight-ton bogie open goods No 13. This photograph was taken after the original top hung doors were replaced by side hung doors. Note also that the doors in the bogie wagon are off centre. *(L&GRP)*

Lynton & Barnstaple Railway. Working Time Table.

JUNE, 1908, or until further notice.

DOWN	1 arr	1 dep (a.m.)	2 Mondays only arr	2 dep (a.m.)	3 arr	3 dep (a.m.)	4 arr	4 dep (p.m.)	5 arr	5 dep (p.m.)	6 Fridays only arr	6 dep (p.m.)	SUNDAYS arr	SUNDAYS dep (a.m.)
Barnstaple (Pilton Yd / Town)	6 7	6E5 / 6 20	8 47	8E45 / 9 5	10 2 (See Note A)	10E0 / 10 30	12 20	12E18 / 12 38	4 17	4L15 / 4 40	See Note J	5 33	7 17	7E15 / 7 30
Snapper		6 30		9 15		10 40		12 48		4 50		5 43		7 41
Chelfham	6 39	6 40	9 24	9 25	10 49	10 50	12 57	12 58	5 0 (X No. 4 up)	5 1	5 52	5 53	7 51	7 52
Bratton	6 55	6 57 (X No. 1 up)	9 40	9 42 (X No. 1 up)	11 4	11 5	1 12 (X No. 3 up)	1 13	5 16	5 17	6 8	6 9	8 6	8 7
Blackmoor	7 15	7 18	9 59	10 0	11 22 (X No. 2 up Mons. only)	11 23	1 30	1 31	5 34	5 35	6 26	6 27	8 25	8 26
Parracombe		7 30		10 12		11 35		1 43		5 47		6 39		8 38
Woody Bay	7 36	7 38	10 18	10 19	11 41	11 42	1 49	1 50	5 53	5 55	6 45 (X No. 5 up)	6 47	8 44	8 46
LYNTON	7 53		10 34		11 57		2 4		6 10		7 2		9 2	

86

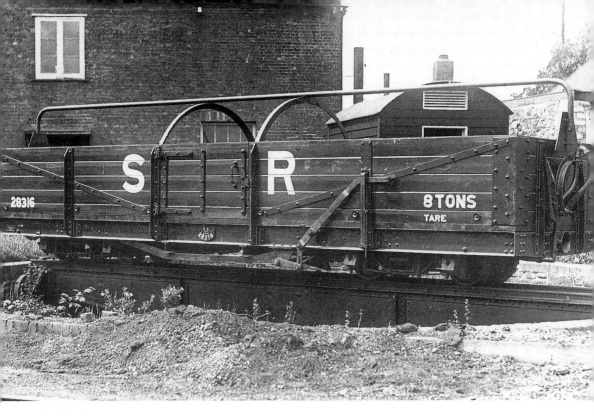

Above: The Southern added four bogie open wagons at the same time as the Howard vans. Here No 28316 (brand new) stands on the turntable at Pilton with the Lynton & Barnstaple offices behind.

(H. G. W. Household)

TRAFFIC

Below: A transfer siding at Barnstaple Town was used for the transfer of complete wagon loads. Traffic arriving in smaller quantities by the standard gauge railways and all traffic originating locally was taken by road to Pilton Yard, and loaded there. This photograph, probably taken around the time of World War I, shows a variety of freight stock at Pilton with the goods shed in the background. *(L&GRP)*

Left: Tyers electric tablet apparatus. A drawing of one of the Barnstaple Pilton Bridge tablets appears right.

(R. L. Knight)

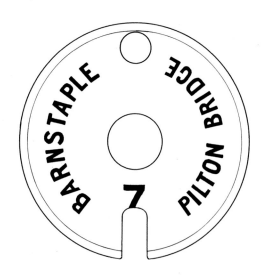

Below: A selection of L&B and SR tickets

CLOSURE

Above and left: Alpha and Omega. The first and the last trains at Pilton before backing down to Barnstaple Town. The train on the left in the 1898 view, with *Yeo*, was the first train. *Exe* headed the second special train, but the coaches shown here were not those used. The last train, in September 1935, has *Lew* and *Yeo*.

(L&GRP; D. E. H. Box)

Right: After closure it was not long before notices advertising sale of equipment and of the freehold property appeared. *(J. G. Dewing)*

DISMANTLEMENT SALE
of the Track, Rolling Stock and Materials of the
LYNTON & BARNSTAPLE RAILWAY

By Order of the Directors of the SOUTHERN RAILWAY CO.
MESSRS.

FULLER, HORSEY,
SONS & CASSELL

WILL SELL BY AUCTION, IN LOTS, AT THE

PILTON DEPOT, BARNSTAPLE, ON
WEDNESDAY, NOVEMBER 13th, 1935

at ELEVEN O'CLOCK precisely,

RAILWAY TRACK, LOCOMOTIVES
ROLLING STOCK & MATERIALS
INCLUDING
16 MILES TRACK
23½-in. GAUGE, 40-lb. F.B. RAILS on 4-ft. 6-in. CREOSOTED SLEEPERS with POINTS AND CROSSINGS
SIGNAL AND TELEGRAPH APPARATUS
FIVE TANK LOCOMOTIVES
Four by MANNING-WARDLE and One by BALDWIN

SEVENTEEN 8-WHEEL PASSENGER CARRIAGES
NINETEEN OPEN GOODS WAGONS (4 TO 8 TONS)
10 COVERED GOODS WAGONS
THREE 8-TON GOODS BRAKE VANS
PLATELAYERS' TROLLEYS, TURNTABLES
PORTABLE CRANES, WEIGHBRIDGES
REPAIR SHOP EQUIPMENT
including LATHES, DRILLING AND GRINDING MACHINES
ENGINEERS' AND SMITHS' TOOLS, TANGYE 14-H.P.
GAS ENGINE, STORES AND MATERIAL, STATION
AND OFFICE FURNITURE AND OTHER EFFECTS

MAY BE VIEWED BY PRODUCTION OF CATALOGUE TO BE OBTAINED OF

F. H. WILLIS, Esq., Secretary to the Southern Railway Co., Waterloo
Station, London, S.E.; or of the Messrs.

FULLER, HORSEY, SONS & CASSELL, Auctioneers,
11, Billiter Square, Fenchurch Street, London, E.C.3

S O U T H E R N   R A I L W A Y.

CIRCULAR NO. 159.

LONDON.

... September, 1935.

INSTRUCTIONS TO ALL CONCERNED.

CLOSING OF THE LYNTON AND BARNSTAPLE LINE.

1.   On and from the 30th September, 1935, the above mentioned Line will be entirely closed.

2.   The Stations and Halts affected are Barnstaple (Pilton Yard), Snapper Halt, Chelfham, Bratton Fleming, Blackmoor, Parracombe Halt, Woody Bay, Caffyn's Halt and Lynton & Lynmouth.

3.   All traffic (Passengers, Parcels and Miscellaneous, Goods, Mineral and Coal Class) to or from places hitherto served by the Lynton and Barnstaple Line, will be dealt with by road services from and to Barnstaple Junction.

4.   All fares and rates recorded with the Stations and Halts which are to be closed require, therefore, to be cancelled and deleted from the Station Lists and Books, on the 30th September, 1935.

5.   Arrangements have been made by the Southern National Omnibus Company to provide road services for passengers between Barnstaple and Lynton, comparable with the existing train facilities.

6.   Stations at present having bookings to the Lynton and Barnstaple Line may continue to issue all descriptions of tickets (except Privilege) through to destination. Except in the case of Cheap Day Tickets, which will be specially advised to the Stations concerned, the fares to be charged will be the appropriate ordinary or reduced fare (as the case may be) to Barnstaple Junction, plus the following fixed amounts for the road portion of the journey, viz:-

To.			Single.	Return.
			s. d.	s. d.
Chelfham	...	...	-/ 7d.	1/2
Bratton Fleming	...	...	-/11d.	1/6
Blackmoor	...	...	1/ 6d.	2/3
Parracombe	...	...	1/ 9d.	2/6
Woody Bay	...	...	1/11d.	3/-
Lynton	...	...	2/ 4d.	3/6

7.   All stocks of "printed" tickets to Lynton and Barnstaple Line Stations must be returned to the Audit Accountant, accompanied by the usual Statements, immediately after 29th September, 1935. Application should at once be made for Printed "Rail and Road" tickets where it is anticipated there will be a fair demand. Issues for which "Printed" tickets are not supplied must be made from the appropriate Blank series.

8.   Parcels and Miscellaneous Traffic (including P.L.A. and D.L.) and unaccompanied Dogs, Bicycles, &c., for places formerly served by the Lynton and Barnstaple Line must be stamped or waybilled to Barnstaple Junction at the rates applicable to that Station. In addition, the appropriate cartage charges shown on attached scale must be collected from sender and placed to Special Debit Book pending receipt of a recharge from Barnstaple Junction. Luggage must not be accepted for conveyance under the C.L. arrangement.

(Cont'd)

9.   Accompanied Dogs, Bicycles, etc., also Excess Luggage, must not be booked beyond Barnstaple Junction. Passengers should be informed that such traffic will be conveyed thence to destination by the Southern National Omnibus Company at their local rates.

10.   Merchandise, Coal & Coke, and other Minerals must be invoiced to Barnstaple Junction at that Station's rates.   In the case of "Paid Home" traffic, the Cartage charges shown on attached scale must be invoiced as "Paid through for Delivery".

11.   Attention is drawn to the fact that on the attached scale two sets of Cartage charges are provided. The appropriate charge must be raised according to whether the traffic is entered at S. to S. or C. and D. rates.

12.   No Cartage charges are to be raised at the Forwarding Stations on Traffic to places formerly served by the Lynton and Barnstaple Line, conveyed by either Goods or Passenger Train under an "Agreed Charges" arrangement; this also applies in the case of "Parcels in Bulk at Flat Rate" traffic.   In all such cases where the "Agreed Charge" or "Flat Rate" does not cover delivery "Home" to destination, the delivery charges will be collected from Consignee or re-charged by Barnstaple Junction to Forwarding Station, according to instructions already issued in regard to Agreed Charging arrangements.

13.   Traffic from Lynton and other places formerly served by the Lynton and Barnstaple Line will be stamped, waybilled or invoiced by Barnstaple Junction.

14.   Stations having correspondence outstanding with Lynton and Barnstaple Line Stations should follow up with Barnstaple Junction. which Station will take over all uncleared matters relating to the Lynton and Barnstaple Line; similarly any questions relating to Undercharges or Overcharges arising hereafter, or disputed items affecting Lynton and Barnstaple Line Stations will be dealt with by Barnstaple Junction.

15.   Further copies of this Circular can be obtained from the Commercial Assistant, London Bridge.

                A. E. MOORE,   E. C. COX,
                    Audit Accountant.   Traffic Manager.

        Superintendent of Operation Reference V.5376
        Commercial Assistant's Reference EP5/451150
        Audit Accountant's Reference A.735

The last train at Lynton hauled by *Yeo* and *Lew* on
Sunday 29 September 1935. The photographs show the
train as it arrived, a scene with the staff posed alongside
the locomotives while the excursionists were in the
town, and the last stationmaster, Stan Liley, on the
platform just before the train left on its final return
working to Barnstaple. *(R. L. Knight)*

The day after the last train ran the stationmaster at Barnstaple Town placed this wreath on the buffer stops. The inscription read 'Perchance it is not dead, but sleepeth'.
(R. L. Knight)